This Log
BELONGS TO

_____

Copyright © 2020
All rights reserved. No part of this publication may be reproduced, distributed, or transmitted in any form or by any means, including photocopying, recording, or other electronic or mechanical methods, without the prior written permission of the publisher, except in the case of brief quotations embodied in critical reviews and certain other noncommercial uses permitted by copyright law.

Movies TO WATCH

TITLE	MAIN ACTOR	GENRE	YEAR	✓

Movies TO WATCH

TITLE	MAIN ACTOR	GENRE	YEAR	✓

Movies TO WATCH

TITLE	MAIN ACTOR	GENRE	YEAR	✓

MY MOVIE Reviews

INDEX PAGE

TITLE	PAGE NO.

MY MOVIE Reviews

INDEX PAGE

TITLE	PAGE NO.

MY MOVIE Reviews

INDEX PAGE	
TITLE	PAGE NO.

MOVIE TITLE 1

DIRECTOR

WRITER

GENRE   DATE RELEASED

PRODUCER

---------- ACTORS ----------

MY REVIEW

---------- HIGHLIGHTS OF THE MOVIE ----------

GREAT QUOTES AND OTHER THINGS TO REMEMBER

---------- OVERALL RATING   1   2   3   4   5 ----------

MOVIE TITLE 2

DIRECTOR

WRITER

GENRE   DATE RELEASED

PRODUCER

--- ACTORS ---

MY REVIEW

--- HIGHLIGHTS OF THE MOVIE ---

GREAT QUOTES AND OTHER THINGS TO REMEMBER

OVERALL RATING   1   2   3   4   5

MOVIE TITLE 3

DIRECTOR

WRITER

GENRE   DATE RELEASED

PRODUCER

--- ACTORS ---

MY REVIEW

--- HIGHLIGHTS OF THE MOVIE ---

GREAT QUOTES AND OTHER THINGS TO REMEMBER

OVERALL RATING   1   2   3   4   5

MOVIE TITLE 4

DIRECTOR

WRITER

GENRE   DATE RELEASED

PRODUCER

--- ACTORS ---

MY REVIEW

--- HIGHLIGHTS OF THE MOVIE ---

GREAT QUOTES AND OTHER THINGS TO REMEMBER

OVERALL RATING   1   2   3   4   5

MOVIE TITLE 5

DIRECTOR

WRITER

GENRE

DATE RELEASED

PRODUCER

--- ACTORS ---

--- MY REVIEW ---

--- HIGHLIGHTS OF THE MOVIE ---

GREAT QUOTES AND OTHER THINGS TO REMEMBER

OVERALL RATING   1   2   3   4   5

MOVIE TITLE 6

DIRECTOR

WRITER

GENRE

DATE RELEASED

PRODUCER

ACTORS

MY REVIEW

HIGHLIGHTS OF THE MOVIE

GREAT QUOTES AND OTHER THINGS TO REMEMBER

OVERALL RATING   1   2   3   4   5

MOVIE TITLE 7

DIRECTOR

WRITER

GENRE   DATE RELEASED

PRODUCER

--- ACTORS ---

--- MY REVIEW ---

--- HIGHLIGHTS OF THE MOVIE ---

GREAT QUOTES AND OTHER THINGS TO REMEMBER

OVERALL RATING   1   2   3   4   5

MOVIE TITLE 8

DIRECTOR

WRITER

GENRE   DATE RELEASED

PRODUCER

———————————— ACTORS ————————————

MY REVIEW

———————— HIGHLIGHTS OF THE MOVIE ————————

GREAT QUOTES AND OTHER THINGS TO REMEMBER

OVERALL RATING   1   2   3   4   5

MOVIE TITLE 9

DIRECTOR

WRITER

GENRE | DATE RELEASED

PRODUCER

--- ACTORS ---

MY REVIEW

--- HIGHLIGHTS OF THE MOVIE ---

GREAT QUOTES AND OTHER THINGS TO REMEMBER

OVERALL RATING   1   2   3   4   5

MOVIE TITLE 10

DIRECTOR

WRITER

GENRE

DATE RELEASED

PRODUCER

ACTORS

MY REVIEW

HIGHLIGHTS OF THE MOVIE

GREAT QUOTES AND OTHER THINGS TO REMEMBER

OVERALL RATING   1   2   3   4   5

MOVIE TITLE 11

DIRECTOR

WRITER

GENRE DATE RELEASED

PRODUCER

--- ACTORS ---

MY REVIEW

--- HIGHLIGHTS OF THE MOVIE ---

GREAT QUOTES AND OTHER THINGS TO REMEMBER

OVERALL RATING 1 2 3 4 5

MOVIE TITLE 12

DIRECTOR

WRITER

GENRE

DATE RELEASED

PRODUCER

ACTORS

MY REVIEW

HIGHLIGHTS OF THE MOVIE

GREAT QUOTES AND OTHER THINGS TO REMEMBER

OVERALL RATING 1 2 3 4 5

MOVIE TITLE 13

DIRECTOR

WRITER

GENRE

DATE RELEASED

PRODUCER

— ACTORS —

MY REVIEW

— HIGHLIGHTS OF THE MOVIE —

GREAT QUOTES AND OTHER THINGS TO REMEMBER

OVERALL RATING   1   2   3   4   5

MOVIE TITLE 14

DIRECTOR

WRITER

GENRE   DATE RELEASED

PRODUCER

--- ACTORS ---

--- MY REVIEW ---

--- HIGHLIGHTS OF THE MOVIE ---

GREAT QUOTES AND OTHER THINGS TO REMEMBER

OVERALL RATING   1   2   3   4   5

MOVIE TITLE 15

DIRECTOR

WRITER

GENRE   DATE RELEASED

PRODUCER

---------- ACTORS ----------

MY REVIEW

---------- HIGHLIGHTS OF THE MOVIE ----------

GREAT QUOTES AND OTHER THINGS TO REMEMBER

---------- OVERALL RATING   1   2   3   4   5 ----------

MOVIE TITLE 16

DIRECTOR

WRITER

GENRE

DATE RELEASED

PRODUCER

--- ACTORS ---

MY REVIEW

--- HIGHLIGHTS OF THE MOVIE ---

GREAT QUOTES AND OTHER THINGS TO REMEMBER

OVERALL RATING   1   2   3   4   5

MOVIE TITLE 17

DIRECTOR

WRITER

GENRE | DATE RELEASED

PRODUCER

--- ACTORS ---

MY REVIEW

--- HIGHLIGHTS OF THE MOVIE ---

GREAT QUOTES AND OTHER THINGS TO REMEMBER

OVERALL RATING 1 2 3 4 5

MOVIE TITLE 18

DIRECTOR

WRITER

GENRE   DATE RELEASED

PRODUCER

---ACTORS---

MY REVIEW

---HIGHLIGHTS OF THE MOVIE---

GREAT QUOTES AND OTHER THINGS TO REMEMBER

OVERALL RATING   1   2   3   4   5

MOVIE TITLE 19

DIRECTOR

WRITER

GENRE   DATE RELEASED

PRODUCER

———————————————— ACTORS ————————————————

MY REVIEW

———————————— HIGHLIGHTS OF THE MOVIE ————————————

GREAT QUOTES AND OTHER THINGS TO REMEMBER

———————— OVERALL RATING   1   2   3   4   5 ————————

MOVIE TITLE 20

DIRECTOR

WRITER

GENRE   DATE RELEASED

PRODUCER

--- ACTORS ---

--- MY REVIEW ---

--- HIGHLIGHTS OF THE MOVIE ---

GREAT QUOTES AND OTHER THINGS TO REMEMBER

OVERALL RATING   1   2   3   4   5

MOVIE TITLE 21

DIRECTOR

WRITER

GENRE   DATE RELEASED

PRODUCER

--- ACTORS ---

MY REVIEW

--- HIGHLIGHTS OF THE MOVIE ---

GREAT QUOTES AND OTHER THINGS TO REMEMBER

OVERALL RATING   1   2   3   4   5

MOVIE TITLE 22

DIRECTOR

WRITER

GENRE — DATE RELEASED

PRODUCER

--- ACTORS ---

MY REVIEW

--- HIGHLIGHTS OF THE MOVIE ---

GREAT QUOTES AND OTHER THINGS TO REMEMBER

OVERALL RATING 1 2 3 4 5

MOVIE TITLE 23

DIRECTOR

WRITER

GENRE   DATE RELEASED

PRODUCER

———————————— ACTORS ————————————

MY REVIEW

———————— HIGHLIGHTS OF THE MOVIE ————————

GREAT QUOTES AND OTHER THINGS TO REMEMBER

———— OVERALL RATING   1   2   3   4   5 ————

MOVIE TITLE 24

DIRECTOR

WRITER

GENRE   DATE RELEASED

PRODUCER

--- ACTORS ---

MY REVIEW

--- HIGHLIGHTS OF THE MOVIE ---

GREAT QUOTES AND OTHER THINGS TO REMEMBER

OVERALL RATING   1   2   3   4   5

MOVIE TITLE 25

DIRECTOR

WRITER

GENRE   DATE RELEASED

PRODUCER

--- ACTORS ---

MY REVIEW

--- HIGHLIGHTS OF THE MOVIE ---

GREAT QUOTES AND OTHER THINGS TO REMEMBER

--- OVERALL RATING   1   2   3   4   5 ---

MOVIE TITLE 26

DIRECTOR

WRITER

GENRE

DATE RELEASED

PRODUCER

— ACTORS —

MY REVIEW

— HIGHLIGHTS OF THE MOVIE —

GREAT QUOTES AND OTHER THINGS TO REMEMBER

OVERALL RATING   1   2   3   4   5

MOVIE TITLE 27

DIRECTOR

WRITER

GENRE   DATE RELEASED

PRODUCER

--- ACTORS ---

MY REVIEW

--- HIGHLIGHTS OF THE MOVIE ---

GREAT QUOTES AND OTHER THINGS TO REMEMBER

OVERALL RATING   1   2   3   4   5

MOVIE TITLE 28

DIRECTOR

WRITER

GENRE   DATE RELEASED

PRODUCER

--- ACTORS ---

MY REVIEW

--- HIGHLIGHTS OF THE MOVIE ---

GREAT QUOTES AND OTHER THINGS TO REMEMBER

OVERALL RATING   1   2   3   4   5

MOVIE TITLE 29

DIRECTOR

WRITER

GENRE   DATE RELEASED

PRODUCER

--- ACTORS ---

MY REVIEW

--- HIGHLIGHTS OF THE MOVIE ---

GREAT QUOTES AND OTHER THINGS TO REMEMBER

--- OVERALL RATING   1   2   3   4   5 ---

MOVIE TITLE 30

DIRECTOR

WRITER

GENRE   DATE RELEASED

PRODUCER

--- ACTORS ---

--- MY REVIEW ---

--- HIGHLIGHTS OF THE MOVIE ---

GREAT QUOTES AND OTHER THINGS TO REMEMBER

OVERALL RATING   1   2   3   4   5

MOVIE TITLE 31

DIRECTOR

WRITER

GENRE   DATE RELEASED

PRODUCER

--- ACTORS ---

MY REVIEW

--- HIGHLIGHTS OF THE MOVIE ---

GREAT QUOTES AND OTHER THINGS TO REMEMBER

OVERALL RATING   1   2   3   4   5

MOVIE TITLE 32

DIRECTOR

WRITER

GENRE

DATE RELEASED

PRODUCER

ACTORS

MY REVIEW

HIGHLIGHTS OF THE MOVIE

GREAT QUOTES AND OTHER THINGS TO REMEMBER

OVERALL RATING 1 2 3 4 5

MOVIE TITLE 33

DIRECTOR

WRITER

GENRE   DATE RELEASED

PRODUCER

--- ACTORS ---

MY REVIEW

--- HIGHLIGHTS OF THE MOVIE ---

GREAT QUOTES AND OTHER THINGS TO REMEMBER

--- OVERALL RATING   1   2   3   4   5 ---

MOVIE TITLE 34

DIRECTOR

WRITER

GENRE　　　　　　　　　　　　DATE RELEASED

PRODUCER

ACTORS

MY REVIEW

HIGHLIGHTS OF THE MOVIE

GREAT QUOTES AND OTHER THINGS TO REMEMBER

OVERALL RATING　1　2　3　4　5

MOVIE TITLE 35

DIRECTOR

WRITER

GENRE   DATE RELEASED

PRODUCER

--- ACTORS ---

MY REVIEW

--- HIGHLIGHTS OF THE MOVIE ---

GREAT QUOTES AND OTHER THINGS TO REMEMBER

--- OVERALL RATING   1   2   3   4   5 ---

MOVIE TITLE 36

DIRECTOR

WRITER

GENRE | DATE RELEASED

PRODUCER

--- ACTORS ---

MY REVIEW

--- HIGHLIGHTS OF THE MOVIE ---

GREAT QUOTES AND OTHER THINGS TO REMEMBER

OVERALL RATING   1   2   3   4   5

MOVIE TITLE 37

DIRECTOR

WRITER

GENRE   DATE RELEASED

PRODUCER

--- ACTORS ---

MY REVIEW

--- HIGHLIGHTS OF THE MOVIE ---

GREAT QUOTES AND OTHER THINGS TO REMEMBER

OVERALL RATING   1   2   3   4   5

MOVIE TITLE 38

DIRECTOR

WRITER

GENRE

DATE RELEASED

PRODUCER

--- ACTORS ---

--- MY REVIEW ---

--- HIGHLIGHTS OF THE MOVIE ---

GREAT QUOTES AND OTHER THINGS TO REMEMBER

OVERALL RATING   1   2   3   4   5

MOVIE TITLE 39

DIRECTOR

WRITER

GENRE   DATE RELEASED

PRODUCER

--- ACTORS ---

MY REVIEW

--- HIGHLIGHTS OF THE MOVIE ---

GREAT QUOTES AND OTHER THINGS TO REMEMBER

--- OVERALL RATING   1   2   3   4   5 ---

MOVIE TITLE 40

DIRECTOR

WRITER

GENRE

DATE RELEASED

PRODUCER

ACTORS

MY REVIEW

HIGHLIGHTS OF THE MOVIE

GREAT QUOTES AND OTHER THINGS TO REMEMBER

OVERALL RATING   1   2   3   4   5

MOVIE TITLE 41

DIRECTOR

WRITER

GENRE					DATE RELEASED

PRODUCER

--- ACTORS ---

--- MY REVIEW ---

--- HIGHLIGHTS OF THE MOVIE ---

GREAT QUOTES AND OTHER THINGS TO REMEMBER

OVERALL RATING   1   2   3   4   5

MOVIE TITLE 42

DIRECTOR

WRITER

GENRE   DATE RELEASED

PRODUCER

--- ACTORS ---

MY REVIEW

--- HIGHLIGHTS OF THE MOVIE ---

GREAT QUOTES AND OTHER THINGS TO REMEMBER

OVERALL RATING   1   2   3   4   5

MOVIE TITLE 43

DIRECTOR

WRITER

GENRE   DATE RELEASED

PRODUCER

--- ACTORS ---

MY REVIEW

--- HIGHLIGHTS OF THE MOVIE ---

GREAT QUOTES AND OTHER THINGS TO REMEMBER

--- OVERALL RATING   1   2   3   4   5 ---

MOVIE TITLE 44

DIRECTOR

WRITER

GENRE

DATE RELEASED

PRODUCER

ACTORS

MY REVIEW

HIGHLIGHTS OF THE MOVIE

GREAT QUOTES AND OTHER THINGS TO REMEMBER

OVERALL RATING   1   2   3   4   5

MOVIE TITLE 45

DIRECTOR

WRITER

GENRE   DATE RELEASED

PRODUCER

---------- ACTORS ----------

MY REVIEW

---------- HIGHLIGHTS OF THE MOVIE ----------

GREAT QUOTES AND OTHER THINGS TO REMEMBER

OVERALL RATING   1   2   3   4   5

MOVIE TITLE 46

DIRECTOR

WRITER

GENRE

DATE RELEASED

PRODUCER

---ACTORS---

MY REVIEW

---HIGHLIGHTS OF THE MOVIE---

GREAT QUOTES AND OTHER THINGS TO REMEMBER

OVERALL RATING   1   2   3   4   5

MOVIE TITLE 47

DIRECTOR

WRITER

GENRE   DATE RELEASED

PRODUCER

---------- ACTORS ----------

MY REVIEW

---------- HIGHLIGHTS OF THE MOVIE ----------

GREAT QUOTES AND OTHER THINGS TO REMEMBER

OVERALL RATING   1   2   3   4   5

MOVIE TITLE 48

DIRECTOR

WRITER

GENRE

DATE RELEASED

PRODUCER

ACTORS

MY REVIEW

HIGHLIGHTS OF THE MOVIE

GREAT QUOTES AND OTHER THINGS TO REMEMBER

OVERALL RATING   1   2   3   4   5

MOVIE TITLE 49

DIRECTOR

WRITER

GENRE   DATE RELEASED

PRODUCER

―――――――――――――― ACTORS ――――――――――――――

MY REVIEW

―――――――――― HIGHLIGHTS OF THE MOVIE ――――――――――

GREAT QUOTES AND OTHER THINGS TO REMEMBER

―――――――― OVERALL RATING   1   2   3   4   5 ――――――――

MOVIE TITLE 50

DIRECTOR

WRITER

GENRE   DATE RELEASED

PRODUCER

ACTORS

MY REVIEW

HIGHLIGHTS OF THE MOVIE

GREAT QUOTES AND OTHER THINGS TO REMEMBER

OVERALL RATING   1   2   3   4   5

MOVIE TITLE 51

DIRECTOR

WRITER

GENRE   DATE RELEASED

PRODUCER

---------- ACTORS ----------

MY REVIEW

---------- HIGHLIGHTS OF THE MOVIE ----------

GREAT QUOTES AND OTHER THINGS TO REMEMBER

---------- OVERALL RATING   1   2   3   4   5 ----------

MOVIE TITLE 52

DIRECTOR

WRITER

GENRE | DATE RELEASED

PRODUCER

ACTORS

MY REVIEW

HIGHLIGHTS OF THE MOVIE

GREAT QUOTES AND OTHER THINGS TO REMEMBER

OVERALL RATING 1 2 3 4 5

MOVIE TITLE 53

DIRECTOR

WRITER

GENRE   DATE RELEASED

PRODUCER

--- ACTORS ---

MY REVIEW

--- HIGHLIGHTS OF THE MOVIE ---

GREAT QUOTES AND OTHER THINGS TO REMEMBER

--- OVERALL RATING   1   2   3   4   5 ---

MOVIE TITLE 54

DIRECTOR

WRITER

GENRE

DATE RELEASED

PRODUCER

--- ACTORS ---

MY REVIEW

--- HIGHLIGHTS OF THE MOVIE ---

GREAT QUOTES AND OTHER THINGS TO REMEMBER

OVERALL RATING   1   2   3   4   5

MOVIE TITLE 55

DIRECTOR

WRITER

GENRE   DATE RELEASED

PRODUCER

——— ACTORS ———

MY REVIEW

——— HIGHLIGHTS OF THE MOVIE ———

GREAT QUOTES AND OTHER THINGS TO REMEMBER

——— OVERALL RATING   1   2   3   4   5 ———

MOVIE TITLE 56

DIRECTOR

WRITER

GENRE

DATE RELEASED

PRODUCER

---- ACTORS ----

MY REVIEW

---- HIGHLIGHTS OF THE MOVIE ----

GREAT QUOTES AND OTHER THINGS TO REMEMBER

OVERALL RATING   1   2   3   4   5

MOVIE TITLE 57

DIRECTOR

WRITER

GENRE **DATE RELEASED**

PRODUCER

--- ACTORS ---

MY REVIEW

--- HIGHLIGHTS OF THE MOVIE ---

GREAT QUOTES AND OTHER THINGS TO REMEMBER

--- OVERALL RATING   1   2   3   4   5 ---

MOVIE TITLE 58

DIRECTOR

WRITER

GENRE   DATE RELEASED

PRODUCER

---------- ACTORS ----------

MY REVIEW

---------- HIGHLIGHTS OF THE MOVIE ----------

GREAT QUOTES AND OTHER THINGS TO REMEMBER

OVERALL RATING   1   2   3   4   5

MOVIE TITLE 59

DIRECTOR

WRITER

GENRE						DATE RELEASED

PRODUCER

--- ACTORS ---

--- MY REVIEW ---

--- HIGHLIGHTS OF THE MOVIE ---

GREAT QUOTES AND OTHER THINGS TO REMEMBER

OVERALL RATING   1   2   3   4   5

MOVIE TITLE 60

DIRECTOR

WRITER

GENRE | DATE RELEASED

PRODUCER

--- ACTORS ---

MY REVIEW

--- HIGHLIGHTS OF THE MOVIE ---

GREAT QUOTES AND OTHER THINGS TO REMEMBER

OVERALL RATING   1   2   3   4   5

MOVIE TITLE 61

DIRECTOR

WRITER

GENRE					DATE RELEASED

PRODUCER

--- ACTORS ---

MY REVIEW

--- HIGHLIGHTS OF THE MOVIE ---

GREAT QUOTES AND OTHER THINGS TO REMEMBER

OVERALL RATING   1   2   3   4   5

MOVIE TITLE 62

DIRECTOR

WRITER

GENRE

DATE RELEASED

PRODUCER

--- ACTORS ---

MY REVIEW

--- HIGHLIGHTS OF THE MOVIE ---

GREAT QUOTES AND OTHER THINGS TO REMEMBER

--- OVERALL RATING --- 1 2 3 4 5 ---

MOVIE TITLE 63

DIRECTOR

WRITER

GENRE   DATE RELEASED

PRODUCER

--- ACTORS ---

MY REVIEW

--- HIGHLIGHTS OF THE MOVIE ---

GREAT QUOTES AND OTHER THINGS TO REMEMBER

OVERALL RATING   1   2   3   4   5

MOVIE TITLE 64

DIRECTOR

WRITER

GENRE   DATE RELEASED

PRODUCER

---ACTORS---

MY REVIEW

---HIGHLIGHTS OF THE MOVIE---

GREAT QUOTES AND OTHER THINGS TO REMEMBER

OVERALL RATING   1   2   3   4   5

MOVIE TITLE 65

DIRECTOR

WRITER

GENRE	DATE RELEASED

PRODUCER

--- ACTORS ---

MY REVIEW

--- HIGHLIGHTS OF THE MOVIE ---

GREAT QUOTES AND OTHER THINGS TO REMEMBER

OVERALL RATING 1 2 3 4 5

MOVIE TITLE 66

DIRECTOR

WRITER

GENRE | DATE RELEASED

PRODUCER

--- ACTORS ---

--- MY REVIEW ---

--- HIGHLIGHTS OF THE MOVIE ---

GREAT QUOTES AND OTHER THINGS TO REMEMBER

OVERALL RATING 1 2 3 4 5

MOVIE TITLE 67

DIRECTOR

WRITER

GENRE   DATE RELEASED

PRODUCER

--- ACTORS ---

MY REVIEW

--- HIGHLIGHTS OF THE MOVIE ---

GREAT QUOTES AND OTHER THINGS TO REMEMBER

--- OVERALL RATING   1   2   3   4   5 ---

MOVIE TITLE 68

DIRECTOR

WRITER

GENRE

DATE RELEASED

PRODUCER

ACTORS

MY REVIEW

HIGHLIGHTS OF THE MOVIE

GREAT QUOTES AND OTHER THINGS TO REMEMBER

OVERALL RATING   1   2   3   4   5

MOVIE TITLE 69

DIRECTOR

WRITER

GENRE   DATE RELEASED

PRODUCER

--- ACTORS ---

MY REVIEW

--- HIGHLIGHTS OF THE MOVIE ---

GREAT QUOTES AND OTHER THINGS TO REMEMBER

OVERALL RATING   1   2   3   4   5

MOVIE TITLE 70

DIRECTOR

WRITER

GENRE   DATE RELEASED

PRODUCER

--- ACTORS ---

MY REVIEW

--- HIGHLIGHTS OF THE MOVIE ---

GREAT QUOTES AND OTHER THINGS TO REMEMBER

OVERALL RATING   1   2   3   4   5

MOVIE TITLE 71

DIRECTOR

WRITER

GENRE   DATE RELEASED

PRODUCER

--- ACTORS ---

--- MY REVIEW ---

--- HIGHLIGHTS OF THE MOVIE ---

GREAT QUOTES AND OTHER THINGS TO REMEMBER

OVERALL RATING   1   2   3   4   5

MOVIE TITLE 72

DIRECTOR

WRITER

GENRE | DATE RELEASED

PRODUCER

--- ACTORS ---

MY REVIEW

--- HIGHLIGHTS OF THE MOVIE ---

GREAT QUOTES AND OTHER THINGS TO REMEMBER

OVERALL RATING 1 2 3 4 5

MOVIE TITLE 73

DIRECTOR

WRITER

GENRE | DATE RELEASED

PRODUCER

---------- ACTORS ----------

MY REVIEW

---------- HIGHLIGHTS OF THE MOVIE ----------

GREAT QUOTES AND OTHER THINGS TO REMEMBER

---------- OVERALL RATING 1 2 3 4 5 ----------

MOVIE TITLE 74

DIRECTOR

WRITER

GENRE   DATE RELEASED

PRODUCER

--- ACTORS ---

MY REVIEW

--- HIGHLIGHTS OF THE MOVIE ---

GREAT QUOTES AND OTHER THINGS TO REMEMBER

OVERALL RATING   1   2   3   4   5

MOVIE TITLE 75

DIRECTOR

WRITER

GENRE   DATE RELEASED

PRODUCER

──────────────── ACTORS ────────────────

MY REVIEW

──────────── HIGHLIGHTS OF THE MOVIE ────────────

GREAT QUOTES AND OTHER THINGS TO REMEMBER

──────── OVERALL RATING   1   2   3   4   5 ────────

MOVIE TITLE 76

DIRECTOR

WRITER

GENRE

DATE RELEASED

PRODUCER

---— ACTORS ---—

---— MY REVIEW ---—

---— HIGHLIGHTS OF THE MOVIE ---—

GREAT QUOTES AND OTHER THINGS TO REMEMBER

OVERALL RATING   1   2   3   4   5

MOVIE TITLE 77

DIRECTOR

WRITER

GENRE   DATE RELEASED

PRODUCER

--- ACTORS ---

MY REVIEW

--- HIGHLIGHTS OF THE MOVIE ---

GREAT QUOTES AND OTHER THINGS TO REMEMBER

--- OVERALL RATING   1   2   3   4   5 ---

MOVIE TITLE 78

DIRECTOR

WRITER

GENRE   DATE RELEASED

PRODUCER

--- ACTORS ---

MY REVIEW

--- HIGHLIGHTS OF THE MOVIE ---

GREAT QUOTES AND OTHER THINGS TO REMEMBER

--- OVERALL RATING   1   2   3   4   5 ---

MOVIE TITLE 79

DIRECTOR

WRITER

GENRE   DATE RELEASED

PRODUCER

——————————— ACTORS ———————————

MY REVIEW

——————— HIGHLIGHTS OF THE MOVIE ———————

GREAT QUOTES AND OTHER THINGS TO REMEMBER

——————— OVERALL RATING 1 2 3 4 5 ———————

MOVIE TITLE 80

DIRECTOR

WRITER

GENRE

DATE RELEASED

PRODUCER

--- ACTORS ---

MY REVIEW

--- HIGHLIGHTS OF THE MOVIE ---

GREAT QUOTES AND OTHER THINGS TO REMEMBER

OVERALL RATING   1   2   3   4   5

MOVIE TITLE 81

DIRECTOR

WRITER

GENRE　　　　　　　　　　　　DATE RELEASED

PRODUCER

--- ACTORS ---

MY REVIEW

--- HIGHLIGHTS OF THE MOVIE ---

GREAT QUOTES AND OTHER THINGS TO REMEMBER

--- OVERALL RATING   1   2   3   4   5 ---

MOVIE TITLE 82

DIRECTOR

WRITER

GENRE

DATE RELEASED

PRODUCER

---------- ACTORS ----------

MY REVIEW

---------- HIGHLIGHTS OF THE MOVIE ----------

GREAT QUOTES AND OTHER THINGS TO REMEMBER

---------- OVERALL RATING   1   2   3   4   5 ----------

MOVIE TITLE 83

DIRECTOR

WRITER

GENRE | DATE RELEASED

PRODUCER

--- ACTORS ---

MY REVIEW

--- HIGHLIGHTS OF THE MOVIE ---

GREAT QUOTES AND OTHER THINGS TO REMEMBER

OVERALL RATING   1   2   3   4   5

MOVIE TITLE 84

DIRECTOR

WRITER

GENRE

DATE RELEASED

PRODUCER

ACTORS

MY REVIEW

HIGHLIGHTS OF THE MOVIE

GREAT QUOTES AND OTHER THINGS TO REMEMBER

OVERALL RATING   1   2   3   4   5

MOVIE TITLE 85

DIRECTOR

WRITER

GENRE   DATE RELEASED

PRODUCER

---------- ACTORS ----------

MY REVIEW

---------- HIGHLIGHTS OF THE MOVIE ----------

GREAT QUOTES AND OTHER THINGS TO REMEMBER

OVERALL RATING   1   2   3   4   5

MOVIE TITLE 86

DIRECTOR

WRITER

GENRE

DATE RELEASED

PRODUCER

--- ACTORS ---

MY REVIEW

--- HIGHLIGHTS OF THE MOVIE ---

GREAT QUOTES AND OTHER THINGS TO REMEMBER

OVERALL RATING   1   2   3   4   5

MOVIE TITLE 87

DIRECTOR

WRITER

GENRE | DATE RELEASED

PRODUCER

--- ACTORS ---

MY REVIEW

--- HIGHLIGHTS OF THE MOVIE ---

GREAT QUOTES AND OTHER THINGS TO REMEMBER

--- OVERALL RATING 1 2 3 4 5 ---

MOVIE TITLE 88

DIRECTOR

WRITER

GENRE   DATE RELEASED

PRODUCER

--- ACTORS ---

MY REVIEW

--- HIGHLIGHTS OF THE MOVIE ---

GREAT QUOTES AND OTHER THINGS TO REMEMBER

OVERALL RATING   1   2   3   4   5

MOVIE TITLE 89

DIRECTOR

WRITER

GENRE   DATE RELEASED

PRODUCER

--- ACTORS ---

MY REVIEW

--- HIGHLIGHTS OF THE MOVIE ---

GREAT QUOTES AND OTHER THINGS TO REMEMBER

--- OVERALL RATING   1   2   3   4   5 ---

MOVIE TITLE 90

DIRECTOR

WRITER

GENRE   DATE RELEASED

PRODUCER

ACTORS

MY REVIEW

HIGHLIGHTS OF THE MOVIE

GREAT QUOTES AND OTHER THINGS TO REMEMBER

OVERALL RATING   1   2   3   4   5

MOVIE TITLE 91

DIRECTOR

WRITER

GENRE | DATE RELEASED

PRODUCER

--- ACTORS ---

MY REVIEW

--- HIGHLIGHTS OF THE MOVIE ---

GREAT QUOTES AND OTHER THINGS TO REMEMBER

OVERALL RATING   1   2   3   4   5

MOVIE TITLE 92

DIRECTOR

WRITER

GENRE   DATE RELEASED

PRODUCER

--- ACTORS ---

MY REVIEW

--- HIGHLIGHTS OF THE MOVIE ---

GREAT QUOTES AND OTHER THINGS TO REMEMBER

OVERALL RATING   1   2   3   4   5

MOVIE TITLE 93

DIRECTOR

WRITER

GENRE   DATE RELEASED

PRODUCER

--- ACTORS ---

MY REVIEW

--- HIGHLIGHTS OF THE MOVIE ---

GREAT QUOTES AND OTHER THINGS TO REMEMBER

OVERALL RATING   1   2   3   4   5

MOVIE TITLE 94

DIRECTOR

WRITER

GENRE　　　　　　　　　　　　　DATE RELEASED

PRODUCER

--- ACTORS ---

MY REVIEW

--- HIGHLIGHTS OF THE MOVIE ---

GREAT QUOTES AND OTHER THINGS TO REMEMBER

OVERALL RATING　1　2　3　4　5

MOVIE TITLE 95

DIRECTOR

WRITER

GENRE   DATE RELEASED

PRODUCER

--- ACTORS ---

--- MY REVIEW ---

--- HIGHLIGHTS OF THE MOVIE ---

GREAT QUOTES AND OTHER THINGS TO REMEMBER

OVERALL RATING   1   2   3   4   5

MOVIE TITLE 96

DIRECTOR

WRITER

GENRE | DATE RELEASED

PRODUCER

--- ACTORS ---

MY REVIEW

--- HIGHLIGHTS OF THE MOVIE ---

GREAT QUOTES AND OTHER THINGS TO REMEMBER

OVERALL RATING   1   2   3   4   5

MOVIE TITLE 97

DIRECTOR

WRITER

GENRE   DATE RELEASED

PRODUCER

--- ACTORS ---

MY REVIEW

--- HIGHLIGHTS OF THE MOVIE ---

GREAT QUOTES AND OTHER THINGS TO REMEMBER

--- OVERALL RATING   1   2   3   4   5 ---

MOVIE TITLE 98

DIRECTOR

WRITER

GENRE | DATE RELEASED

PRODUCER

ACTORS

MY REVIEW

HIGHLIGHTS OF THE MOVIE

GREAT QUOTES AND OTHER THINGS TO REMEMBER

OVERALL RATING   1   2   3   4   5

MOVIE TITLE 99

DIRECTOR

WRITER

GENRE   DATE RELEASED

PRODUCER

———————————————— ACTORS ————————————————

MY REVIEW

———————————————— HIGHLIGHTS OF THE MOVIE ————————————————

GREAT QUOTES AND OTHER THINGS TO REMEMBER

———————————— OVERALL RATING   1   2   3   4   5 ————————————

MOVIE TITLE 100

DIRECTOR

WRITER

GENRE

DATE RELEASED

PRODUCER

--- ACTORS ---

--- MY REVIEW ---

--- HIGHLIGHTS OF THE MOVIE ---

GREAT QUOTES AND OTHER THINGS TO REMEMBER

OVERALL RATING   1   2   3   4   5

MOVIE TITLE 101

DIRECTOR

WRITER

GENRE   DATE RELEASED

PRODUCER

--- ACTORS ---

MY REVIEW

--- HIGHLIGHTS OF THE MOVIE ---

GREAT QUOTES AND OTHER THINGS TO REMEMBER

--- OVERALL RATING   1   2   3   4   5 ---

MOVIE TITLE 102

DIRECTOR

WRITER

GENRE   DATE RELEASED

PRODUCER

--- ACTORS ---

MY REVIEW

--- HIGHLIGHTS OF THE MOVIE ---

GREAT QUOTES AND OTHER THINGS TO REMEMBER

OVERALL RATING   1   2   3   4   5

MOVIE TITLE 103

DIRECTOR

WRITER

GENRE   DATE RELEASED

PRODUCER

--- ACTORS ---

MY REVIEW

--- HIGHLIGHTS OF THE MOVIE ---

GREAT QUOTES AND OTHER THINGS TO REMEMBER

--- OVERALL RATING   1   2   3   4   5 ---

MOVIE TITLE 104

DIRECTOR

WRITER

GENRE   DATE RELEASED

PRODUCER

---------- ACTORS ----------

MY REVIEW

---------- HIGHLIGHTS OF THE MOVIE ----------

GREAT QUOTES AND OTHER THINGS TO REMEMBER

---------- OVERALL RATING   1   2   3   4   5 ----------

MOVIE TITLE 105

DIRECTOR

WRITER

GENRE   DATE RELEASED

PRODUCER

--- ACTORS ---

--- MY REVIEW ---

--- HIGHLIGHTS OF THE MOVIE ---

GREAT QUOTES AND OTHER THINGS TO REMEMBER

OVERALL RATING   1   2   3   4   5

Printed in Great Britain
by Amazon